920

Twenty
CAMPAIGNERS FOR CHANGE

Nigel Hunter

Illustrated by Edward Mortelmans

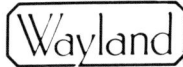

Twenty Names

Twenty Names in Medicine
Twenty Names in Modern Literature
Twenty Campaigners for Change
Twenty Names in Pop Music
Twenty Names in Classical Music
Twenty Names in Sport
Twenty Novelists
Twenty Inventors
Twenty Names in Art
Twenty Explorers
Twenty Names in Crime
Twenty Poets and Playwrights
Twenty Tyrants

Editor: Rosemary Ashley

First published in 1987 by
Wayland (Publishers) Limited,
61 Western Road, Hove,
East Sussex BN3 1JD, England

© Copyright 1987 Wayland (Publishers) Ltd

British Library Cataloguing in Publication Data
Hunter, Nigel
    Twenty campaigners for change.
    1. Biography
    I. Title II. Mortelmans, Edward
    920'.02   CT104

    ISBN 1–85210–136–9

Phototypeset by Kalligraphics Ltd, Redhill, Surrey
Printed in Italy by G. Canale & C.S.p.A., Turin
Bound in Britain at The Bath Press, Avon

Contents

The quest for 'Utopia'

In 1516 Sir Thomas More published a book that described an imaginary island of perfect contentment and justice. The book's title, and the island's name, was *Utopia*. This word has since passed into the English language as the term for an ideal society. But its Greek root carries a sting – when translated, 'utopia' really means 'nowhere'.

Nowhere is society perfect. But changes and improvements do sometimes take place. The institution of slavery for example, which existed in many parts of the world for thousands of years, and seemed (to the slave owners at least) quite 'natural', is now largely abolished, and recognized for the abomination it really was. Sometimes social improvements take many generations to achieve; sometimes they occur over the course of just a few years. It depends how deep-rooted the problems are.

Right *Symbols of 20th Century campaigns – left to right – Women's Suffrage, Anti-nuclear and Polish Workers Solidarity.*

No individual can ever achieve fundamental changes alone. It takes a communal effort on the part of many people. But occasionally, certain individuals can be credited with a leading role. This book singles out twenty men and women who have been responsible for stimulating others towards various kinds of social change. They all wrote, spoke or acted in ways calculated to bring about a more just or harmonious society; but few can be classed as simple 'utopians', aspiring to a perfect society. Most knew only too well 'the unhappy thought that human kind cannot bear very much harmony', as Germaine Greer has put it.

There are no 'violent revolutionaries' and no political rulers among them. They are simply people concerned with poverty, war, exploitation and oppression. They all had a commitment to 'change', and they acted with the courage of their convictions for the betterment of all.

1

Thomas Paine

Tom Paine was a writer with one great subject – liberty. He lived during a period of great change, in many respects the dawn of modern times, and he was at the centre of some of the period's most momentous events.

Paine was born in Norfolk, England, in 1737. In 1774 he left to live in America and before long he became a key figure in the movement for American Independence.

In 1777 he wrote a pamphlet, *Common Sense*, in which he urged the Americans to throw off the shackles of British rule. He called for an independent, democratic America; for uncorrupt government based on the will of the people, which would be an example to the whole world. Paine's fame and influence started to spread as the American Revolution began, and with its triumphant conclusion, the grateful nation awarded him a farm, where he lived comfortably for several years.

1737 born in Thetford, England
1748 works as stay-maker in father's business
1760 becomes Customs and Excise officer
1774 travels to America
1776 *Common Sense* published; American War of Independence begins
1777 appointed Secretary to
–79 Congress' Committee
1779 Secretary to Clerk of
–81 the Pennsylvania Assembly
1791 *Rights of Man* published
–92 in England; flees to France under threat of arrest
1792 member of the French
–93 Convention
1794 imprisoned in Paris
1796 *Age of Reason* published
1809 dies in New York

Paine's book *The Rights of Man*, was written in defence of the principles of the French Revolution of 1789. He wrote it while visiting his native England, and its publication resulted in his being convicted of high treason. Fortunately, by then he had escaped to France. The book's message called for elected republican government with the abolition of old aristocratic privileges. 'Men are born, and always continue, free and equal with respect to their rights,' it stated; '. . . and these rights are liberty, property, security, and resistance of oppression.'

Paine was at first welcomed in France. But before long, because he spoke against the execution of Louis XVI, he was imprisoned. Only luck (a misplaced chalk mark on his cell door) saved him from the guillotine. In prison he completed his last great book, *The Age of Reason*, which criticized the Bible and established religion. This offended many people. He died in New York, impoverished and almost forgotten: a bitter fate for someone who contributed so much.

Above *The French National Assembly – the post-revolutionary governing body of France.*

Below (left) *Paine wrote much of his last book as a prisoner of the Jacobins, the most radical of the French revolutionaries.*
(Right) *Paine, 'the Apostle of Liberty' was a strong influence on America's founding Fathers.*

2
Mary Wollstonecraft

Mary Wollstonecraft was a forerunner of the women's liberation movement. Like many others in Britain at that time, she was sympathetic towards the aims of the French Revolution of 1789, although it did not challenge the unequal position of men and women in society.

Mary was born in London. She worked as a lady's companion and governess – then she started to write. Her book *A Vindication of the Rights of Women* was published in 1792. With its appeal to 'reason' and the notion of 'rights', it was very much a book of its time, but to many people it was a scandalous work. The book examined the situations of men and women in society, comparing the position of women to that of slaves, and referring to the lack of female education which led to their loss of economic independence. Few careers were open to women at that time – as a writer, Mary herself was a rare exception. The

1759 born in London
1778 becomes 'lady's companion
1783 sets up girls' school in London.
1788 *Original Stories from Real Life* published
1790 *Vindication of the Rights of Man* published
1792 *Vindication of the Rights of Woman* published
1794 *A Historical View of the French Revolution* published; daughter Fanny born
1795 returns to Britain; travels to Scandinavia
1797 marries William Godwin; daughter Mary (later Mary Shelley, author of *Frankenstein*) born; dies ten days after childbirth

poorest earned a scant living through the dreary toil of agricultural or industrial labour; while 'gentlewomen' were trained only to be the docile, obedient servants of their husbands. Such conditions degraded both men and women, and wasted half humanity's potential.

Mary Wollstonecraft was already famous as the author of a book on 'the rights of man' (preceding Thomas Paine's better-known work by several months). Her book on the 'rights of women', and her subsequent life, made her a notorious figure. She was much admired in France, and visited Paris – only to witness the 'Terror' following the French Revolution, during which some of her friends were guillotined. In 1794 she gave birth to an illegitimate daughter, and, abandoned by the father, she attempted suicide. She later married the writer William Godwin and bore him a daughter in 1897. She died soon after, but her call for women's rights still echoes down the ages.

Above *French nobility imprisoned during the 'Terror', which followed the French Revolution of 1789.*

Below *Women had little power in eighteenth century society – and women workers perhaps had least of all.*

3
Robert Owen

Robert Owen owned cotton mills at New Lanark, in Scotland, and organized his business unlike any other mill-owner of the time. The whole enterprise was more of an experiment in community living than a business. To begin with, he built a village for the workers. They were provided with good housing, and clean, healthy surroundings; and they could buy nourishing food cheaply in the village shops.

There was also education for all children up to the age of twelve. This in itself was unusual because most children started work considerably younger in those days. Teaching methods at New Lanark were very progressive for the time. Corporal punishment was banned; the children were kindly spoken to and instructed to 'make each other happy'. Believing that people's characters are formed by their environment and education, Owen used his business profits to improve conditions even further. The workers were also

Below *Owen's enlightened approach to education was far ahead of its time.*

allowed a say in all decisions affecting their lives. New Lanark was visited and much admired by many leading political figures of the day.

Owen published his ideas in books and pamphlets, and talked about them during travels to France, Switzerland and Germany. He recommended the formation of 'villages of co-operation', made up of 200 to 300 families, where members would work according to their ability, for the good of the whole community. He also spoke out strongly against religion, declaring it to be a barrier to progress.

Communities based on 'Owenite' principles were started in several places. The best known was called New Harmony, which Owen himself set up in the USA in 1824. Unfortunately, not everyone connected with it was as idealistic, or as well-intentioned, as its founder, and the scheme collapsed a few years later. Owen then became involved in the newly-formed co-operative and trade union movements that were beginning to grow in Britain.

Above *The 'model community' of New Lanark.*

1771	born in Newtown, Wales
1780	becomes shop assistant
1790	cotton-mill manager, Manchester
1800	begins New Lanark 'experiment'
1813	*A New View of Society* published
1816	*Address to the Inhabitants of New Lanark* published
1818	travels in Europe
1824	travels to USA, establishes New Harmony
1828	New Harmony fails
1829	withdraws from New Lanark
1832	lectures, writes, becomes involved with co-operative and trade union movements
1858	dies in Newtown

4
Frances Wright

Frances Wright was born in Dundee, in Scotland, but she spent most of her life in the USA, campaigning for social change. She first 'discovered' the USA when she was sixteen, after reading a book about the American Revolution and the ideals of liberty that inspired it.

When she first went to the USA in 1818, she did not find the ideal society she had dreamed of. She saw men, women and children being bought and sold as slaves – people with no more legal rights than horses or dogs. She expressed her feelings about this in a book entitled *Views of Society and Manners in America*. Then she went to live in France where she became a friend of Lafayette, an aristocrat who had fought for the Americans against the British, and who had later served in the French revolutionary government.

In 1824 she returned to the USA, continuing her campaign against slavery. She visited former

1795	born in Dundee, Scotland
1818	first visit to USA
1821	*Views of Society and Manners in America* published
1821	lives in Paris
1824	returns to USA; visits New Harmony; sets up Nashoba commune
1826	visits Britain after Nashoba fails
1829	starts *New Enquirer* with Robert Dale Owen
1834 –37	lecture tours, 'Fanny Wright Societies' founded
1852	dies in Cincinnati

Right   *To Frances Wright slavery was the worst of many social wrongs – against all the principles that the USA stood for.*

presidents Thomas Jefferson and James Madison, both founding fathers of the American constitution, seeking their support. Then, inspired by Robert Owen's New Harmony, she purchased a plot of land in Tennessee, and bought twenty-six people out of slavery, establishing them in a commune there. But her experiment failed and she paid for the former slaves to travel to the free republic of Haiti.

Frances Wright wrote and lectured against slavery, and in favour of women's rights. She also campaigned against religion and the influence of the Church in politics, and against repressive education. She spoke against the death penalty for crime and promoted birth-control and freer divorce laws (she and her husband, a French doctor, were separated). 'Fanny Wright societies' emerged, campaigning on socialist principles, and leading to a progressive workers' movement in the USA. For many years she remained a compelling speaker, and a vital influence for social change.

Above *A slave auction in a southern state of the USA in the mid-nineteenth century.*

5
Henry David Thoreau

Henry Thoreau was an American writer of the mid-nineteenth century – and a philosophical rebel against his society. His masterpiece, *Walden; Or, Life in the Woods*, was based on the two years that he spent living alone in a simple hut near Concord in Massachussetts. The book is mainly about his feelings about nature and the damaging effects of modern civilization.

But another, much shorter, work has had perhaps even more influence than *Walden*. *Civil Disobedience* was an essay written with a particular social abuse in mind: slavery, which still existed in many southern states of the USA. The essay concerns government, law and moral conscience. In it, Thoreau argues that when law and conscience are in conflict, it is conscience, rather than law, that should be obeyed. 'It is not desireable to cultivate a respect for the law, so much as

For two years Thoreau lived beside Walden Pond, studying nature and meditating on the problems of civilized life.

for the right,' he maintains.

'I cannot for an instant recognize that political organization as *my* government which is the *slave's* government also,' Thoreau stated. He believed that refusal to support such a government was the only choice for a person with honest moral principles. He himself withheld his taxes, and went to prison for it, but much to his annoyance a friend paid up for him, and he was jailed for only one night.

Civil Disobedience is a classic statement about 'dissent' – about the right of individuals morally to judge their governments, and, in certain circumstances, to defy the authority of government by breaking the law. The essay has inspired countless campaigners for change in the years since Thoreau's death. Gandhi and Martin Luther King, in particular, praised it for its ideas: it justified their actions, and in action, civil disobedience has proved a powerful force.

1817	born in Concord, Massachusetts
1833	studies at Harvard
–37	University
1838	establishes school, teaches in Concord
1840	first essays and poems published
1845	lives at Walden
–47	Pond
1849	*Civil Disobedience* and *A Week on the Concord and Merrimack Rivers* published
1854	*Walden* published
1862	dies in Concord

6
Frederick Douglass

Frederick Douglass was born a slave in the USA's 'Deep South'. At about the age of twenty, he escaped to the North. He became a leading opponent of slavery – a powerful speaker and writer in the 'abolitionist' cause. In later life he was a respected champion of equal rights for everyone, regardless of race or sex.

In 1845 he wrote a book about his life as a slave, exposing the routine brutality, the 'gross fraud and inhumanity' of the system. In it Douglass told how he had learned to read and write (education for slaves was against the law) and of his growing feelings of rebellion and desire for freedom. But he could say nothing about his escape: for the sake of other fugitives, details of the 'underground railroad' to the North had to remain a secret.

Even in the northern states, escaped slaves risked being captured and sent back to their

1818	born on a plantation in Talbot County, Maryland, USA
1825	sent to be 'house slave' in Baltimore
1833	returned to plantation
1838	sent to work in shipyard in Baltimore; second escape attempt succeeds; lives in New York, then Boston
1841	joins abolitionist movement
1845	*Narrative of the Life of Frederick Douglass, An American Slave* published
1847	begins *The North Star*
1859	flees to Britain after abolitionist raid at Harper's Ferry fails
1861–5	US Civil War
1877	Marshall for the District of Columbia
1889	Minister and General Consul to Haiti
1895	dies

southern 'owners'. Douglass was advised to go abroad, and he went to live in Britain for two years. There he joined forces with various reform groups, speaking out not only against slavery, but also against alcohol (another form of bondage, he believed), and in favour of women's rights and 'home rule' for Ireland. Back in New York, he founded an abolitionist newspaper, the *North Star*, with help from some of his British supporters, who also paid for him to become a legally free man.

Throughout the 1850s he campaigned for abolition, but it was not until the North and South went to war in 1861 that the institution of slavery was seriously threatened. Douglass's influence helped to persuade President Lincoln that it had to be ended. Douglass also recruited black volunteers to serve in the northern army, on equal terms with white volunteers. The war ended slavery; but the battle for full civil rights for black Americans was only just beginning.

Above *Abolitionists being expelled from a meeting in Boston in 1860.*

Below *The escape route from the southern states helped many slaves to reach the North.*

7

Annie Besant

Annie Besant's life went through many changes. She grew up in London as Annie Wood, and married Frank Besant, an Anglican clergyman, at the age of twenty. Her public career began five years later, when her marriage broke down. At that time she was writing a series of anti-religious pamphlets – thoughtful essays criticizing the teachings of the Church.

She then started writing for a 'free-thinking' journal, the *National Reformer*. Her articles dealt with political and social issues, and continued her arguments against the Bible. She became a celebrated, although very controversial, public speaker. In 1877 she and Charles Bradlaugh, a dynamic politician, published a book about birth-control, and were prosecuted for obscenity. They were found 'not guilty', on appeal, but as an 'unfit mother' Annie later lost the custody of her daughter.

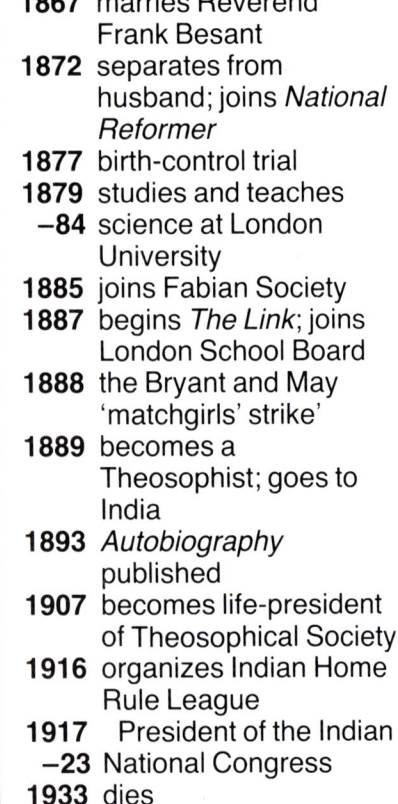

1847 born in London
1867 marries Reverend Frank Besant
1872 separates from husband; joins *National Reformer*
1877 birth-control trial
1879 studies and teaches
−84 science at London University
1885 joins Fabian Society
1887 begins *The Link*; joins London School Board
1888 the Bryant and May 'matchgirls' strike'
1889 becomes a Theosophist; goes to India
1893 *Autobiography* published
1907 becomes life-president of Theosophical Society
1916 organizes Indian Home Rule League
1917 President of the Indian
−23 National Congress
1933 dies

For some years she was a science student at London University, one of the first women to study there. Then she joined the Fabian Society, a socialist reform group which included such figures as writer George Bernard Shaw. She founded a campaigning newspaper, the *Link*, which promoted such causes as the emancipation of women and trade union rights, and discussed the issues of child-labour, education, factory conditions and the Irish problem. In 1888 she helped organize a successful strike for improved conditions by the women workers at a match factory, where cancer was an occupational hazard.

In her forties Annie Besant discovered Theosophy, a religious philosophy claiming to derive from Buddhism and Hinduism. She became Theosophy's international leader, and spent the remaining part of her life in India. Her last cause was Indian self-rule. She became a political leader in the Independence struggle, and a national heroine to the Indian people.

Above *The matchmakers' strike committee, 1888.*

Below *Her work for trade-unionism and other causes made Annie Besant one of the leading public figures of her time.*

8
Jane Addams

Jane Addams was for many years one of the best known and most admired women in the world – some people even called her 'Saint Jane'. She was a lifelong campaigner for social justice, peace and human rights. Her base was a social settlement in Chicago named Hull House.

She founded Hull House in 1889. It was a community and residential centre in one of the poorest, most run-down areas of the city, where many of the local people were hard-pressed immigrants. Jane's purpose was 'to feed the hungry and care for the sick . . . give pleasure to the young, comfort the aged' – and provide a place where people could meet. Eventually, the settlement occupied thirteen buildings, generously donated by one of her supporters. It became a model for many other similar projects throughout the USA.

Up to two thousand people came to Hull House every day, where they were offered opportunities

1860 born in Cedarville, Illinois, USA
1881 studies at Women's
–82 Medical College, Illinois
1883 travels in Europe
1889 founds Hull House in Chicago
1910 *Twenty Years at Hull House* published
1915 President of Women's International League for Peace and Freedom; European 'peace congress' in Holland
1930 *The Second Twenty Years at Hull House* published
1931 co-winner of the Nobel Peace Prize: donates award money to the Women's Peace Party
1935 dies in Chicago

not readily available elsewhere. There were social clubs, lectures and readings, an art gallery, museum, theatre, music school and gymnasium. Research was carried out into local conditions, and campaigns were organized for many social and political reforms. Jane herself led campaigns for better housing and sanitation, for school playgrounds, juvenile courts, and an improved educational system. She upheld the rights of exploited workers – often women and children – and fought hard against political corruption.

Soon after the First World War broke out in 1914, she became president of the newly formed 'Women's International League for Peace and Freedom'. She led fifty American women to a peace congress in Holland, attended by delegates from most of the major European countries. But the women's petitions to various governments had no effect. For a few years, patriots scorned her for her anti-war campaigning. But in 1931, she received the Nobel Peace Prize for all her work.

Above *The arrival of the US Peace Mission in Holland in 1915 – Jane Addams is in the front, 2nd from right.*

Below *Jane spent her life working to improve social conditions in her native country and promoting international peace.*

9
Sylvia Pankhurst

Sylvia Pankhurst was the most radical member of a famous campaigning family. With her mother Emmeline and sister Christabel, she helped to lead the British Suffragette movement, which fought determinedly and courageously for the right of women to vote in democratic elections. But she believed that 'votes for women' was only part of a much wider struggle for political freedom and justice. Her sympathies lay with the poor and oppressed of all countries.

The Suffragettes began with protest meetings, demonstrations, petitions and reasoned argument. When these failed to have any effect on the government, they started to make their point through violent actions. These were always directed against property rather than people. Between 1909 and 1914, over a thousand women served prison sentences for offences connected with the suffragette movement, the Pankhursts being jailed many times. In prison, the Suffragettes often went on hunger-strike, and many under-

1882	born in Manchester, England
1903	Emmeline Pankhurst founds the Women's Social and Political Union; start of the Suffrage campaign
1912	begins campaigning among the women workers of London's East End
1914	start of 1st World War; begins war-relief and peace work
1918	women over thirty given the vote in Britain
1919	serves six months in prison for socialist 'sedition'
1936	begins *New Times*, relating to Ethiopia
1944	first visit to Ethiopia
1954	emigrates to Ethiopia
1958	*A Cultural History of Ethiopia* published
1960	dies in Addis Ababa

went forcible feeding. This was little less than torture, but to win the vote many were willing to suffer and even die if necessary.

The First World War seemed to Emmeline and Christabel a chance for women to gain respect – and ultimately, the vote – by becoming indispensable to the war-effort. Sylvia, however, did not agree with the war. She was a pacifist and a socialist. She worked in London's East End, helping women workers and their children. She hoped to build the foundations of a movement for radical change in the future.

After the War, women aged over thirty were at last given the vote. But Sylvia's socialist campaigning continued. She became involved with the fate of Ethiopia, which was invaded by Fascist Italy in 1935. Her anti-Fascist newspaper, *New Times*, kept people in touch with events throughout Europe and North Africa. After the Second World War she emigrated to Ethiopia. She helped with various valuable social projects in that country, and became a much-respected friend of the developing countries of the world.

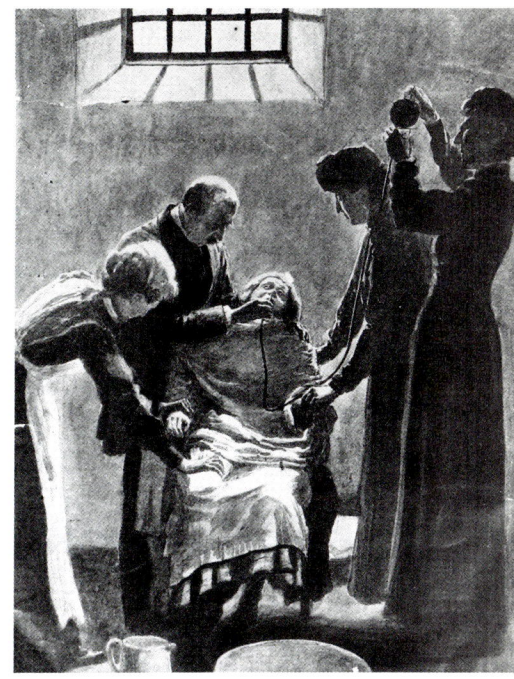

Above *A suffragette hunger-striker being force-fed in prison.*

Below *'Shoulder to shoulder and friend by friend', women demanded the vote.*

10
Mahatma Gandhi

Mahatma Gandhi opposed all forms of injustice and oppression – his guiding principle was 'non-violence'. He was a social reformer, a political leader and an outstanding moral and religious teacher. He taught by example, as well as by speech and the written word; and he led a great nation to independence.

Gandhi's first campaigns took place in South Africa, where he went in 1893. He directed his campaigns against laws that restricted the rights of people in the South African Indian community. He set to work, calling public meetings, organizing groups, arranging petitions and writing to the press.

Gandhi developed a form of public protest involving non-violent acts of civil disobedience by large numbers of people. For deliberately breaking certain laws, he and many thousand others were frequently imprisoned, but eventually they succeeded in having most of these laws repealed. He called this form of protest

1869	born in Porbandar, India
1888 −91	studies law in England
1893 −1914	works and campaigns for Indians' rights in South Africa
1915	returns to India; tours the country, speaking on reforms and national self-rule
1920	becomes President of the All-India Home Rule League and leading voice in the Indian National Congress; begins Campaign of 'passive resistance' to British rule
1931	attends Round Table Conference in London
1932 −42	campaigns continuously, ending with imprisonment during the Second World War
1947	Indian Independence; fasts against inter-religious violence
1948	assassinated in Delhi

satyagraha, which means 'love-force' or 'truth-power' – 'Love' and 'Truth', for Gandhi, being identified with God.

After returning to his native India in 1915, he became a leader in the movement for national self-rule. This meant not just a struggle against the British authorities, but also a struggle for unity among the Indian people themselves. Gandhi toured the country, speaking against religious divisions, against the Hindu caste system, and in favour of equality for women.

The Independence struggle involved many millions of people in countless courageous and disciplined acts of defiance, inspired by Gandhi who himself was imprisoned several times. At government conferences, he spoke for peace and justice for the Indian people. When violence between Muslims and Hindus broke out in India he fasted in protest until it stopped. His home was a self-sufficient commune, or *ashram* – by choice, he owned almost nothing. His assassination, six months after independence, seemed to many people a blow against humanity.

Above   *Gandhi toured the villages of India before Independence, urging toleration between Muslims and Hindus.*

Below   *For Gandhi and his followers, the spinning-wheel became a symbol of India's unity and desire for independence.*

11

Bertrand Russell

Bertrand Russell was born into a British aristocratic family. He was a distinguished mathematician and philosopher who became a popular hero. His political activities were based on 'an unbearable pity for the suffering of mankind.' He explained on his ninetieth birthday, 'I have a very simple creed: that life and joy and beauty are better than dusty death.' He was born in the era of cannons and cavalry and died well into the age of nuclear weapons.

In 1907 Russell stood for Parliament, as the candidate for Women's Suffrage. He was not elected, but his campaign brought valuable publicity to the cause. As a pacifist, he campaigned against the First World War, through newspaper articles, speeches and personal contact with leading politicians. He served six months in prison for a statement which the British Government considered particularly damaging to the wartime cause.

1872	born in North Wales
1890	studies at Cambridge University
1907	stands for Parliament as Suffrage candidate
1914	start of 1st World War
1915	campaigns against war
1918	imprisoned for anti-war statement
1920	visits USSR and China
1924	lecture tour in USA
1927	founds Beacon Hill school with Dora Russell
1950	awarded Nobel Prize for Literature
1955	issues anti-nuclear manifesto with Albert Einstein: start of anti-nuclear conferences
1958	Campaign for Nuclear Disarmament founded: appointed first President
1960	founds 'Committee of 100' – militant civil disobedience wing of CND
1961	imprisoned for civil disobedience
1970	dies

Russell welcomed the Russian Revolution of 1917 as a great political advance, but after visiting the country in 1920, he described Soviet Communism as 'tyrannical bureaucracy'. But he also objected to the expanding 'empire of American finance'. He became a controversial figure in the USA, not only for his political views, but also for his views on sexual freedom and education.

The 'Cold War' between East and West following the Second World War dominated Russell's later life. In speeches, broadcasts and manifestos, he called passionately for peace. Nuclear war, he said, could destroy humanity. He became President of the newly-formed Campaign for Nuclear Disarmament (CND), and took part in many mass protests. At eighty-nine he went to prison for a week, for advocating anti-nuclear civil disobedience. Until his death he continued to be involved in humanitarian causes. He died, however, believing that he had made only 'a puny effort against vast forces'.

Above *A march in memory of the victims of the first atomic bombing in Japan.*

Below *In his old age, Russell became the world's leading advocate of nuclear disarmament.*

12
Martin Luther King

Martin Luther King led the campaign for civil rights for black Americans and gave his life for the cause. Like Gandhi, he fought injustice and oppression through non-violent protest. He fought for new laws, and for adequate enforcement of existing laws, to ensure political and social equality for black Americans. It was a struggle to overcome racial prejudice and the violence that accompanied it.

King grew up in one of the former slave states, in the USA's 'Deep South', where white attitudes to blacks had hardly changed since the Civil War (1861–5). Segregation laws kept the races apart, and denied equal opportunities to black people. They had the worst of everything: housing, jobs, education and transport. Only a few, including King's own family, were moderately well-off. And all black people lived with the threat of sudden violence from a fanatical organization called the Ku Klux Klan.

1929 born in Atlanta, Georgia
1947 ordained as Christian minister
1948 continues studies in
−53 Philadelphia and Boston
1954 pastor in Montgomery, Alabama, civil rights campaign begins
1956 black people boycott buses in Montgomery
1957 'Prayer Pilgrimage' to Washington, seeking equal rights; travels to Africa and Europe
1963 anti-segregation campaign in Birmingham, Alabama; the 'Great March on Washington'
1964 awarded Nobel Peace Prize; Civil Rights Act passed
1968 assassinated in Memphis, Tennessee

He worked from the heart of the black community, the Christian Church. As a Baptist minister, he developed a passionate form of public speaking, which he turned to good account in the civil rights campaign.

There were many dramatic events during the campaign, involving thousands of people – marches, boycotts, sit-ins. Television news publicized the issues world-wide. Civil rights demonstrators were often confronted by crowds of hostile whites, and sometimes the police action against them was terrifying. Many suffered, and some even died for the cause. But gradually, over the years, these brave campaigners forced through various changes in the law.

King's most famous speech was in 1963, at a huge civil rights rally in Washington: 'I have a dream,' he said; and he described a future world free from hatred and violence. The following year he was awarded the Nobel Peace Prize. But his assassination, in 1968, left his shattered followers with a great deal still to do.

Above *King and his wife Coretta at the head of a civil rights march in 1965.*

Below *Martin Luther King inspired a movement which gave black Americans new hope for the future.*

13

Joan Baez

Joan Baez is a well-known American singer and songwriter, with many best-selling records to her name. For twenty-five years, she has also been known as a campaigner for non-violence and human rights. Her philosophy of non-violence was inspired by Gandhi, and her first public involvement was with Martin Luther King's civil rights movement, which began in 1954.

Civil Rights prompted a general revival of the 'folk-protest' tradition in singing early in the 1960s and many new songs were heard at marches and demonstrations. Some of these were about events of the times; and others, like *We Shall Overcome*, were to inspire the campaigners. Joan took part in many protest rallies, including the great march on Washington in 1963. Once, she took a little black girl into a newly de-segregated southern school, pushing her way through a mob of angry whites.

1941 born in Staten Island, New York State
1959 sings at the Newport Folk Festival,
1960 involved in civil rights movement
1963 Vietnam War escalates: involved in anti-war protests
1967 imprisoned for three weeks for anti-'draft' activities
1972 visits North Vietnam as guest of 'Committee for Solidarity with the American People'
1973 joins Amnesty International
1977 works with refugees in
−79 South-East Asia; founds Humanitas
1985 opens the American 'Live Aid' concert

Joan gave concerts to raise money for the civil rights movement and for welfare organizations. Her pacifist principles led her to become a leading protester against American involvement in the Vietnam War. She announced that she was withholding the portion of her taxes that would go to military purposes, and she encouraged resistance to the 'draft' (compulsory military service). In 1965 she founded the Institute for the Study of Non-violence, in California.

She was briefly imprisoned for civil disobedience against the War in 1967, but until the War's end she continued her opposition, speaking out for peace at rallies and concerts, and through interviews and recordings. Later, she joined the advisory council of Amnesty International, which helps political prisoners, and founded Humanitas, an international human rights organization. She has also worked for the welfare of South-East Asian refugees. 'There is only one tribe,' she has said – 'Arm up with love'.

Above *A Christmas Eve concert at Notre Dame Cathedral in Paris in 1980 – dedicated 'to the children of the world'.*

Left *As an anti-war protester, Joan Baez remained undeterred by her arrest in 1967.*

31

14
E. F. Schumacher

Fritz Schumacher was an economist who dealt in human as well as financial values. He believed that modern industrial society was leading humankind to destruction, putting too much emphasis on short-term material gain, and not enough on the quality of life. He argued that society ignored people's spiritual needs and led to dissatisfaction, poverty, war, and the ecological ruin of the Earth. What was needed, he said, was a different attitude, and complete re-organization: economics 'as if people mattered'.

Schumacher was born in Germany but left to settle in Britain after Hitler's rise to power. It was only towards the end of his life that his ideas became widely known. They were based on many years of personal and professional experience. For thirty years he had been one of the world's foremost economists and an advisor to industry and governments. He had also been a keen student of philosophy, and religion – the world's

1911 born in Berlin
1930 studies economics at Oxford University
1934 leaves Nazi Germany
−37 to work in London
1939 2nd World War: interned
−45 as 'enemy alien'; later appointed to Oxford Institute of Statistics
1945 British official in post-
−47 war Germany
1955 develops theories of 'non-violent economics'
1965 founds 'Intermediate Technology Development Group'
1966 visits Third World
−73 countries, advising government leaders
1973 *Small Is Beautiful* published
1977 *A Guide for the Perplexed* published; dies abroad during lecture-tour

'traditional wisdom', as he called it. At one time he almost became a Buddhist, but eventually turned to Roman Catholicism.

Schumacher believed that Western society had abandoned responsibility for the future. The West's industrial development was based on the rapid exploitation of non-renewable sources of energy – coal, oil and gas; and nuclear energy involved the stockpiling, for thousands of years ahead, of vast amounts of dangerous waste. Pollution of lakes and forests put humankind 'out of balance with nature', he warned.

In his book *Small is Beautiful*, Schumacher quoted Gandhi: 'Earth provides enough to satisfy every man's need, but not for every man's greed.' He argued that large-scale businesses needed to be collectively owned and controlled, and that a simpler technology, adapted to local conditions, was better for developing countries than Western-style technology. Some people considered him a 'crank'; but as he said, 'A crank is a piece of simple technology that creates revolutions.'

Fritz Schumacher believed that industrial pollution is not only dangerous but also symptomatic of many underlying ills in modern society.

15
Germaine Greer

Germaine Greer is a feminist writer and social commentator who first became well-known in the early 1970s. She was born in Australia, but has lived mainly in Britain and rural Italy since the mid-1960s. Soon after her arrival in Britain she became involved with the 'underground' sub-culture of the time, which led many people to suppose she was a leader of the 'permissive society'. Yet, she says, this was a mistake: in fact, she was 'one of its bitterest opponents'.

She published her first book, *The Female Eunuch*, in 1970. This was a lively account of the ways in which Western society oppressed women and how it tended to define women in ways that made them out to be passive sexual objects 'for the use and appreciation of men.' She argued that this process of demeaning women worked through various social 'myths', such as 'the

1939	born in Melbourne, Australia
1960 –64	studies literature at Melbourne and Sydney Universities
1964	studies at Cambridge University, England
1968 –73	teaches at Warwick University, writes for *Oz*, *Suck* and the *Sunday Times*; *The Female Eunuch* published (1970)
1979	*The Obstacle Race* published
1984	*Sex and Destiny* published
1975	attends Conference of UN's International Women's Year, Mexico City
1984 –85	visits to Brazil, Cuba and Ethiopia

Right *Greer's contacts with women in the developing world have led her to ask disturbing questions about the impact of Western policies.*

middle-class myth of love and marriage'. She claimed that such repression actually enslaved both women and men, and that if women liberated themselves, this would also benefit men.

Her book *The Obstacle Race* was about women painters of the past, and how traditional art-history has managed to overlook their achievements. It was part of a general feminist project to recover women's 'lost' history. Her next book, *Sex and Destiny*, argued that, through a misplaced belief in Western superiority, Western attitudes to the developing countries are threatening to overwhelm and ruin traditional non-Western societies.

Recently Germaine Greer has travelled to Brazil, Cuba and Ethiopia to research local conditions from a feminist point of view. Her hopes for the future are based on the adoption of 'sisterly' values of care and co-operation. In her writings, perhaps, are some of the seeds of change.

Above *Germaine Greer's writings have made her a controversial public figure.*

16
Andrei Sakharov

Andrei Sakharov is a prominent Soviet dissident, a courageous campaigner for human rights, international co-operation and disarmament. For many years he was forced to live in 'internal exile' in the city of Gorky, under the constant watch of the KGB (the Soviet secret police). In December 1986 he was permitted to return to Moscow.

Sakharov was once an official state hero of the USSR. He was a leading member of the team that developed the country's first hydrogen bomb, in 1953. But the nuclear weapons programme involved tests that led to radioactive fall-out and pollution. He first challenged the Soviet authorities with his campaign against weapons-testing, in the early 1960s. Then he became active in wide-ranging political and social protest.

At first, Sakharov's efforts were directed mainly towards senior Soviet government officials. But his opinions also began to circulate in illegal *samizdat* publications, which soon found their way to the West. He called for freedom of thought

Below *Sakharov's release in December 1986 – and the hundreds more which followed – have raised hopes for significant changes in the USSR.*

and expression in the USSR, and for international co-operation to prevent nuclear catastrophe and environmental pollution, and to help the developing countries of the world.

With two friends, he founded the Moscow Human Rights Committee in 1970. The Committee supported oppressed minorities in their battles against the authorities; campaigned against the death penalty in the USSR; gave aid to other critics of the Soviet regime and publicized the plight of political prisoners. Through meetings with foreign journalists and politicians, he built up his contacts with the West.

Sakharov was denounced by his scientific colleagues and fiercely attacked in the Soviet press. His family and friends also suffered considerable harassment. But in 1975, as a 'spokesman for the conscience of mankind', he was awarded the Nobel Peace Prize. However, his human rights activities eventually led to his arrest in 1980. It remains to be seen how his recent release from internal exile will affect Sakharov's courageous campaigning.

1921	born in USSR
1945	nuclear physicist
1953	helps develop H-bomb
1957	begins anti-testing campaign
1966	protests against 'anti-Soviet slander' law
1968	writings circulated in *samizdat* form in USSR, published in the West as *Sakharov Speaks*
1970	Moscow Human Rights Committee formed
1973	denounced by Soviet Academy of Science
1975	awarded Nobel Peace Prize. *My Country and the World* (Western publication only)
1978	*Alarm and Hope* published in West
1980	arrested and sent to 'internal exile' in Gorky
1984 –85	'hunger-strikes' to achieve Western medical treatment for wife Yelena
1986	released from internal exile

Left *The plight of thousands of 'prisoners of conscience' in Soviet prison camps has been publicized by Sakharov's courageous campaigning.*

17
Lech Walesa

For a brief time in the early 1980s Lech Walesa embodied all the best hopes of Poland. He was the people's champion, their chief spokesman in a quest for reform and human rights, based on the 'free trade union' movement.

In July 1980 there were workers' strikes all across Poland, in response to a sudden rise in meat prices. The strikes were not reported in the government-controlled press, but news spread through the activities of a dissident organization called KOR (Workers' Defence Committee). KOR had contacts in most of the factories, transport-services and mines, and distributed its own newspaper.

By August the strikes had spread to the port of Gdansk. Walesa, an electrician, had been employed at the Lenin Shipyard there, but had been dismissed and imprisoned in previous years for demanding workers' rights. The strikers demanded his reinstatement, and he joined them in their occupation of the shipyard. He became

1943	born in Popow, Poland
1956	price-rises: workers' unrest in Poznan
1970	'bread-riots' in Gdansk; becomes involved with the workers' committee
1976	is sacked for his activities, and imprisoned
1980	meat prices provoke widespread strikes; becomes workers' leader in Gdansk; Solidarity formed; meets Communist Party leader
1981	Solidarity allowed radio and TV time; 4-hour strike by 13 million; protests over food-shortages; meeting with Jaruzelski and Cardinal Glemp; martial Law declared
1982	released after ten months' detention
1983	awarded Nobel Peace Prize

their chief negotiator, and Gdansk became the centre of events.

Soon the workers were demanding fundamental changes, including an end to government censorship of the media, and the right to form trade unions independent of Communist Party control. At the shipyard the Polish government signed an historic agreement. The new unions combined to form 'Solidarity', and over the next fifteen months the great mass of the people rallied under its scarlet banner.

Poland's Soviet-bloc allies were horrified by what seemed an increasing challenge to Communist Party rule. Then Solidarity called for free elections in Poland, and similar free trade unions in other East European countries. The prime-minister, General Jaruzelski, was appointed the new Polish Communist Party leader, and head of state; and in December 1981, he ordered an army takeover. Walesa and thousands of Solidarity activists were arrested, and the union was suppressed. His Nobel Peace Prize in 1983 could hardly have compensated for this defeat.

Above *Lech Walesa kneels in prayer before resumed Solidarity debates at Gdansk in September 1981.*

Far left *Solidarity's memorial to shipyard workers killed during protests in 1970. (Right) Martial law, the sad end.*

18

E. P. Thompson

Edward Thompson is a leading member of the European peace movement. As a historian, he is well qualified to say, 'We do not live in ordinary times.' He warns that we live in an age of great danger. For humankind, it is a question of change, or perish.

His appeal for a 'nuclear-free zone' in Europe was launched at press conferences held simultaneously in five capital cities, in April 1980. It gained the support of many hundreds of public figures, from politicians and Churchmen, to artists and scientists. The appeal spoke of the 'demented arms race' – of the new, increasingly accurate weapons of the USSR and the USA; and of new military strategies for fighting a 'limited nuclear war' in Europe.

'We are now in great danger,' wrote Thompson; '. . . in a world living always under menace, fear extends through both halves of the European continent.' He called for the defence and extension

Below *Demonstrators block the path of a support convoy as US missiles travel from Greenham Common to Salisbury Plain in England.*

of civil rights in both East and West, and for the opening up of both 'blocs' to the free exchange of ideas, and contact between their citizens. People had to act together to break down the Cold War mentality, and free Europe from nuclear weapons. 'We offer no advantage to either NATO or the Warsaw alliance . . . In working for the peace of Europe we are working for the peace of the world.'

END (European Nuclear Disarmament) was formed to support the activities of peace campaigners throughout the continent of Europe. There was growing opposition to new weapons, such as 'Cruise' and 'SS 20' missiles, that were about to be stationed in various countries. Hundreds of thousands of people joined demonstrations, and protested in many different ways. Nevertheless, the weapons arrived. 'What is needed,' Edward Thompson warns, 'is less "arms control" than control of the political and military leaders who deploy these arms . . . Time,' he insists, 'is not on our side.'

Above *Thomson meets one of his leading opponents, US Defence Secretary Caspar Weinberger.*

1924	born in England
1939 –45	serves in 2nd World War
1946	studies at Cambridge
1950	anti-Korean War protests; *The Making of the English Working Class* published
1958–63	active in CND
1980	*Writing by Candlelight* and *Protest and Survive* published; foundation of END
1981	upsurge of anti-nuclear protest in Europe; and 'freeze' movement in USA
1982	*Zero Option* published
1982	continues to work with END and the world-wide peace movement

19
Desmond Tutu

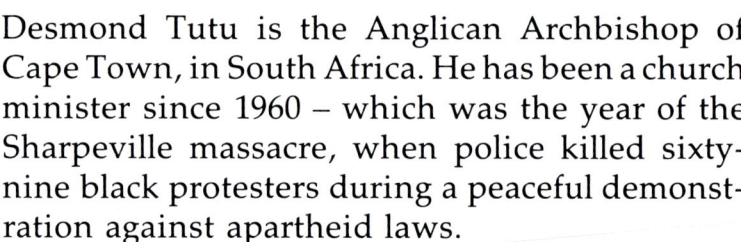

Desmond Tutu is the Anglican Archbishop of Cape Town, in South Africa. He has been a church minister since 1960 – which was the year of the Sharpeville massacre, when police killed sixty-nine black protesters during a peaceful demonstration against apartheid laws.

Apartheid (separate development for different racial groups) is a fact of life in South Africa and still claiming the lives of protesters. Five hundred people, mainly schoolchildren, were killed in Soweto in 1976; and thousands more have lost their lives in a mounting spiral of violence ever since. Under the 'State of Emergency' declared in 1985 by the South African government, news coverage has been restricted and it is difficult to know what is happening in the country.

'The Gospel of Christ is subversive of all injustice and evil,' Tutu teaches: 'The liberator God . . . is always on the side of the exploited and oppressed.' Apartheid maintains white power and privilege; and condemns 'non-whites' to lives of hardship, suffering and insecurity. It is essentially un-Christian, he says. Christianity

Below *Tutu blesses clothes and blankets donated to homeless victims of the effects of apartheid, 1986.*

teaches unity rather than separation – we are all 'children of God'.

Because of pressure from people in the country, and some influence from the outside world, the South African government has introduced reforms. But these are merely 'cosmetic, superficial changes', says Archbishop Tutu. Real change would include voting rights for black people. He supports the release of the African National Congress leader Nelson Mandela, who has been detained in prison for twenty-five years. Tutu's own political role results from actions against such people as Mandela and his wife Winnie being imprisoned, detained without trial, banned or, like the 'Black Consciousness' leader, Steve Biko, simply killed at the hands of the security police.

He calls for negotiations between recognized representatives of the various communities in South Africa, before full-scale civil war breaks out. International economic sanctions will help, he says, despite short-term suffering. 'Desperate people use desperate means,' he warns; 'freedom is certain. But how soon? How bloody must the transition be?'

1931	born in Klerksdorp in Transvaal
1951	studies at Pretoria
–53	Bantu Normal College
1960	ordained in Johannesburg
1962	studies in England;
–66	curacy at St Albans
1967	teaches theology in
–72	South Africa and neighbouring countries
1975	becomes first black Dean of the Anglican Church in South Africa
1976	Soweto protests against 'Bantu' education – 500 killed
1977	appointed General Secretary of the South African Council of Churches
1981	travels to Europe and the USA
1982	*Crying in the Wilderness* published
1984	awarded the Nobel Peace Prize
1985	South African government imposes State of Emergency; pleads for effective sanctions against the South African regime in London

Left *Tutu hands a bible to one of his flock. He teaches 'The liberator God is always on the side of the exploited and oppressed'.*

43

20
Bob Geldof

Bob Geldof was the driving-force behind 'Live Aid', which raised $US100,000,000 for famine relief in Africa in 1985. At meetings with government leaders he frankly condemned official aid policies as scandalous. He was not afraid to speak his mind, and he voiced the opinions of countless ordinary people.

As a teenager in Dublin he spent many nights helping an organization which provided comfort for the city's down-and-outs. After a variety of jobs, he formed the Boomtown Rats with some friends, and they became one of the most successful 'punk' or 'new wave' groups.

In November 1984, turning on the TV news, he saw 'horror on a monumental scale'. In war-torn Ethiopia, millions of people were starving. The dying children's agony even made some newscasters weep. Geldof decided to bring together many of Britain's most popular musicians to record a song he wrote with Midge Ure of

1953 born in Dublin, Eire
1975 forms Boomtown Rats
1976 makes records, tours,
−84 has many hit singles, *Rat Trap, I Don't Like Mondays* etc
1984 forms Band Aid for Ethiopian famine-relief
1985 visits Ethiopia and Sudan, sees effects of famine, and war; meets Mother Teresa; meets government leaders and relief-agency workers; forms Band Aid Trust to administer the Live Aid fund; lobbies in Washington and Strasbourg for improved US and EEC aid policies
1986 receives many awards, autobiography, *Is That It?* published

Ultravox. *Do They Know It's Christmas/Feed The World* by Band Aid sold more copies than any other British single; and since everybody connected with it worked without pay, all profits – £8,000,000 – went to help the starving people of Ethiopia. When he visited the famine areas to decide how the money could best be spent, he saw that the tragedy extended across much of northern Africa.

Bob Geldof then devised a spectacular international appeal. It took determined organization, but finally on 13 July 1985, the world was linked via TV satellite into a true 'global village', and two billion people watched 'Live Aid'. It was a seventeen-hour rock concert centred in London and Philadelphia, featuring many of the world's top stars, and prompting donations from many thousands of people from all walks of life. Similar events, like 'Sport Aid', followed. 'Something', Geldof wrote later, 'had gone right. Cynicism and greed and selfishness had been eliminated for a moment. It felt good.'

Above *The Prince and Princess of Wales among the audience of 90,000 in London to see the Live Aid concert which raised more than £100 million world-wide.*

Below *Geldof's sympathy for the famine victims was matched only by his anger at the complacency of politicians.*

Glossary

Abolitionist Someone who advocated the abolishing of slavery in the USA.

Apartheid The South African government's policy of racial segregation.

Birth-control Methods used to prevent child-bearing.

Bloc A group of countries combined by a common aim.

Caste In Hinduism, the four social 'classes'.

Civil disobedience A refusal to obey laws – a non-violent means of protest or attempting to gain political goals.

Cold War The state of hostility between the Western and the Soviet blocs.

Communist Someone who favours communism – a form of government based on common ownership of goods and resources.

Democratic A political system based on the will of the majority of citizens.

Disarmament The reduction of war weapons by a country or group of countries.

Dissident Someone who disagrees fundamentally with their government's rule.

Ecological To do with the balance of living organisms and the environment.

Fascist Someone who favours fascism – a form of government based on force and suppression of opposition.

Feminist Someone who advocates equal rights for women.

Free-thinking Rejecting religious 'authority'.

Lobby To apply pressure or influence for the passage of a (government) bill.

Manifesto A public declaration of policy.

NATO North Atlantic Treaty Organization.

Obscenity (In law) the state of being depraved or corrupt.

Pacifist Someone who rejects violence or war.

Permissive society People who hold liberal views, particularly on sexual matters.

Radical Favouring fundamental changes in social conditions.

Revolution The overthrow of one form of government in favour of another.

Samizdat A system of secret printing and distribution of banned or dissident literature.

Sanctions Pressure designed to force change, for example, a ban on trade.

Segregation To be set apart from others.

Socialist Favouring socialism – a form of government based on economic equality.

Suffrage The right to vote.

'Underground' A movement in pop music in the 1960s which led to experimentation in other fields, such as fashion and alternative lifestyles.

Warsaw alliance An alliance of Eastern European countries.

Further reading

Alias Papa – a life of Fritz Schumacher by Barbara Wood (Jonathan Cope, 1984)

Annie Besant by Rosemary Dinnage (Penguin, 1986)

Bertrand Russell and His World by Ronald Clark (Thames & Hudson, 1981)

Crying in the Wilderness by Desmond Tutu (H & S Collins/Fount, 1986)

Daybreak, An Autobiography by Joan Baez (MacGibbon, 1970)

Emmeline and Her Daughters by Iris Noble (Bailey Brothers & Swinfen, 1974)

Gandhi by Nigel Hunter (Wayland, Great Lives Series, 1985)

Is That It? by Bob Geldof (Sidgwick and Jackson/Penguin, 1986)

Life and Death of Mary Wollstonecraft by Claire Tomalin (Weidenfeld & Nicolson, 1974)

Martin Luther King by Nigel Hunter (Wayland, 1985)

Protest and Survive by E. P. Thompson (Penguin, 1981)

Robert Owen, Prince of Cotton Spinners ed. J. Butt (David & Charles, 1971)

Index

Picture acknowledgements

BBC Hulton page 21, 23; Mary Evans Picture Library 17, 19; Mansell Collection 11; Popperfoto 37, 41, 42; Topham Picture Library 27, 29, 31, 35, 39, 45; Wayland Picture Library 7, 9, 13.